So You're Thinking About

Contemporary Worship

Tim and Kathy Carson

Chalice Press
St. Louis, Missouri

© Copyright 1997 by Chalice Press

Cover design: Dan Fruend

10 9 8 7 6 5 4 3 2 1   97 98 99 00 01 02

Library of Congress Cataloging–in–Publication Data

Carson, Timothy L.
    So you're thinking about contemporary worship / Tim and
Kathy Carson.
        p. cm.
    ISBN 0-8272-3437-6
    1. Public worship. I. Carson, Kathy. II. Title.
BV15.C38 1997
264–dc21
[264]   97-19597
                                                          CIP

Printed in the United States of America

So
You're
Thinking
About

Contemporary
Worship

For all our friends at

Webster Groves Christian Church

who brought a vision of

contemporary worship

into reality.

Contents

 # $\mathcal{A}$cknowledgments

$\mathcal{S}$everal years ago a small group of leaders and members in our congregation began to dream together about different ways our congregation could engage in worship. From these early dreams and visions the reality of contemporary forms of worship came. We thank the early dreamers, who continue to dream of greater things even still.

The leadership of our congregation is forward-thinking. Even though alternative forms of worship did not appeal to some of our leaders, and they personally preferred a more traditional style of worship, they supported those who did want something different. This is a tribute to their selflessness. But more importantly, our leadership came to understand that to be a church that reaches out to all of those around us, and not just to some, we needed to offer much greater variety and breadth in our worship life. Leaders in our congregation, we salute you!

We also thank the week-in, week-out servants of the church who made the music, set up the worship space, greeted and welcomed, preached, and prayed. You made it happen, and without you would nothing be made that is made! Our *Wind of the Spirit*_{SM} contemporary band has set the tone for everything we have done. The current leadership of the Rev. James Brooks and early contributions by the Rev. Marilyn Druhe have been inspiring.

As always, we thank God for taking us into this time. For the whole church, and for our congregation, this time in history is a transitional one. The fact that huge shifts are occurring within and without the church does not mean, however, that God is somehow absent. To the contrary, the Spirit is continually active in creating a new thing for a new day. God has always supplied our daily needs as we have needed them. In countless ways we are given what we need. And lest we confuse God's provision with our own, the gifts were often provided at the last minute—but they did come!

Finally, we want to thank every church camp counselor or director, retreat leader, or assembly worship team who taught us through example, how Christian worship may be lively, engaging, and inspiring. We are also grateful to all of our pastors of the past and present who brought the creative treasures of heart and soul to the Christian community's worship, and did so with integrity.

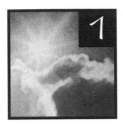

$\mathcal{I}$f the form of public worship is like a ship that carries a precious cargo of the spirit, we know that, through the ages, that ship has taken on different designs for changing times.

In some cases this form has changed in order to reflect a change in theology, such as John Calvin rotating the worshiping position of his congregation inside his church in Geneva ninety degrees, effectively moving the worship focal center to the side of the sanctuary. This made a powerful statement about the nature of the church, the sacraments, and the place of the Word within the community of the faithful.

On the other hand, when Martin Luther adapted the familiar and popular tunes of his day in the service of Christian worship, he did so as an apologetic. He was striving to make contact with the culture toward which the gospel was making its way.

These examples of Calvin and Luther remind us of at least two things. First, form may indeed *modify* the cargo, and we ought not be naive about its ability to do so. Second, form is often altered to *protect* the cargo in the interest of providing safe delivery to a new and formerly unanticipated port.

This book is primarily about the latter—taking the legacy of our best theology and worship to a new port of call. This is a port our ancestors could never have imagined. It is the port of our contemporary world. This port is both like and unlike ports of the past. Its distinctiveness requires a way of worship that, like a scribe of the kingdom, must bring forth the best of the old and the new. And unless the church is willing to sail in a vehicle capable of traveling in such waters, the bread and wine that we stow in our hold will never find their way to those languishing in the spiritual famine of our times.

ONCE UPON A TIME

Like Dorothy making her way toward Oz, and encountering unexpected ones who would accompany her on the way, our journey toward a contemporary worship service began with a few Christians sharing a dream. That small group included pastors and several others who knew that our attempts to reach out to the irreligious or unchurched would be severely limited if we did not offer expanded and divergent worship opportunities. In addition, members *within* the congregation desired a different kind of worship—informal, engaging, intimate, joyful, and presented in a mode which seemed relevant to their lives and experience. As important and meaningful as the traditional worship in our congregation was and still remains, we discovered that in order to remain a living Christian community, we would have to learn from

Christians throughout time from around the world, and also offer something different.

When you are grasped by a powerful new possibility, there is nothing harder than holding back. Impulse often sends us toward our longings with abandon. After first moving forward in a burst of enthusiasm, however, we slowed our pace. In our eagerness to begin, we had set too ambitious of a starting date. We were about to launch prematurely into something *very* difficult to do in congregations with an already-existing worship tradition. Mercifully, we came to view our journey toward a new way of worship as a process that would require much deliberation, preparation, and hard work before we ever held our first service. For this grace of slowing down, we are thankful. Too many congregations have begun their new service prematurely without first doing their homework, clarifying purposes, carefully organizing, and drawing the congregation on board. The fact that so many well-intentioned services have lasted less than six weeks and then quietly died without so much as a decent funeral is testimony enough. This in turn becomes another failure for the congregation and inevitably adds to future resistance in regard to innovation: "Well, you remember what happened when we tried that last fiasco!"

PLOWING THE FIELD, PLANTING THE SEED

Where to begin? Begin by reading, visiting, and attending workshops.

First, read anything you can find on developing

contemporary worship in the congregation. As you do, remember that some of what is shared will not apply to you. Though all congregations are similar at a core level, your congregation, like all congregations, is a special one. It comes with a built-in tradition, history, and personality. Your leadership of the moment has particular views, opinions, and theologies. Because you are unique, you simply cannot directly apply everything that is found. Adaptation will be necessary. Reading just a few pages of the plethora of books published on contemporary worship will have you saying to yourself, "This is written for mega-churches," or "We don't believe that!" or "It might work in that part of the country, but not here...." The key is to identify the key principles and then translate them into your particular setting. You want to create something beautiful before God and among God's people. That beauty will not come because you have made a carbon copy of someone else. Find your own voice, your own style, and your own way. But read, read, read anyway. And then share what you have read with one another.

Second, visit other congregations that are actually doing contemporary worship. Look for what moves you. Ask yourself all the pressing questions:

How does music fit in?
What do they do with the sacraments?
What is the role of the minister?
Is the preaching style different?
Does the worship space enhance or detract from
    this form of worship?

How is Christian community fostered?
Is there room for a sense of mission or cultivating
  discipleship?

When you do visit, go with a small group. This enables you to take your experience back with you and analyze it with the added perception of several points of view. If you can, request a meeting with some of the leadership following the service and ask them to share their story of beginnings. Solicit their advice and counsel. Ask about those bobbles which should be avoided. There are many to avoid like the plague!

Again, resist the temptation to copy directly the service you are attending. If it works, it works for them in their location and setting. If you are an urban congregation, a suburban model might well spell disaster for you. If your church is in a rural area, it might be unwise to attempt to replicate something that works famously well in the inner city. Instead, ask: "What are these Christians doing that powerfully reaches out to those *in their context?*" Identify the basic ingredients, then bake your own casserole.

We have a pastor friend who has a wonderful contemporary service in a part of the world where country music is alive and well. Their service includes some of the very best music from that culture. It connects with them in their place. The same could easily be said of a retirement-oriented church. What would be contemporary worship in that setting? It might be a service that employs some of the very finest big-band, 40s, swing-era jazz around!

Third, let your leadership team attend at least one workshop on contemporary worship in which you are able to hear experienced persons describe their ministry and make suggestions upon it. Such opportunities usually have good time for interaction with others, specific workshops, and ample time for questions.

Talk, talk, talk to each other about it. Remember what has spiritually moved you in contemporary worship services. Take note of what seemed ineffective or theologically fluffy. Don't stop sharing your visions of a church that could be.

You are starting a dynamic journey, not a static one, and one of the keys to your success will be your willingness to constantly re-evaluate and make adjustments along the way. After more than three years of offering contemporary worship in our congregation, we have come to realize that we will never fully arrive at where we want to be; we just keep heading in that direction. The reign of God is here, to be sure, but it is also yet to be!

Do Not Operate in a Vacuum

More than one fine minister, worship committee, or lay leader have fallen victim to the enthusiasm of their own dream. No matter how anxious you may be to begin, do not forget to include the congregation in the process. It matters a great deal that the congregation understands why this is important, that it will not jeopardize other ministries of the church, and that it is not expected that everyone will want to participate.

This is not a time for force-feeding. What you need is the *support* of the leadership in the congregation. I can support something that I know to be important to other members in the church and a doorway to reaching the unchurched without jumping up and down about it myself. Some of our very strongest supporters of contemporary worship in the beginning and at the present time are not church members who attend that service. They are people who love the church and know that the church has always found ways to reach out to every new generation. You will find it very interesting who actually attends the contemporary service after it begins. Some of the younger crowd will continue to attend traditional services. And some of your older adults will become regulars. There is no telling!

When we began the process of taking the proposal for contemporary worship to the congregation, we took it a step at a time, and slowly discussed it in several different key places. Of course, it was a matter of discussion in our worship division for several months. The board chair and church officers discussed all of its ins and outs. The elders of the church[+] dedicated two full elders' meetings to the topic, one of which included a presentation by those advocating for contemporary worship. From those meetings, several key questions emerged as to the effect this might have on other

[+] The elders in the Disciples of Christ comprise the highest office of spiritual leadership for lay persons in the congregation. They preside at the Lord's table, provide spiritual guidance for members, and deliberate on matters that affect the spiritual well-being of the congregation. For Disciples, the elders fulfill one of the aspects of the three-fold New Testament pattern for ministry, the *presbyteroi*.

services and how the location might affect other church programming. All of these questions were taken seriously. The elders brought the wisdom of experience and commitment to the health of the whole congregation. The next step was to bring the whole proposal to our programmatic cabinet of ministries and then the church board. By the time we approached the board, many of those board members had already discussed, considered, and prayed about the matter, because they had been involved earlier in the process. The only thing left was details...plenty of details.

The importance of moving through such a process with the congregation is often overlooked, not only in this particular matter, but in most newly-initiated ministries. Your motivation for involving the congregation should not simply be an attempt to get what you want. It is important because this new worship service needs to *belong to the congregation*. The congregation needs to develop an exciting sense of ownership. More often than not, this has to do with the way in which it is presented. Remember: People resent arriving at a destination without the benefit of taking the trip.

Which way to go? One blended service, with elements of both traditional and contemporary woven together? Or two or more services, each distinct in its own style?

This most difficult question always stands waiting to be asked by any congregation that ventures beyond offering one service each Sunday. Depending on the congregation—its size, location, and membership—one service may seem to be the only option which is available. If we are running fifty in attendance on a Sunday morning, how could we possibly divide into *two* worshiping groups? That is a valid question and an understandable anxiety. If we feel small now, what will it be like after the cell divides?

If the answer to the above question is that the church simply cannot subdivide, the congregation may intentionally add elements to the service that appeal to different persons. This generally can be done if the changes are very modest and keep the same basic form and atmosphere of the service. Churches that attempt this often begin services with more informality and progress toward more formality during the course of the morning. The problem with this approach is that blending styles sometimes ends up pleasing no one, but perhaps disgruntling everyone; no one receives that which is truly gratifying.

The blended service is a possibility, and perhaps the necessary option in a number of circumstances. In our opinion, however, we generally counsel against it. It simply does not meet enough of the identified spiritual needs to be worth either the energy or the conflict. Instead of tinkering with revisions to one service, visionary leadership may instead help the congregation understand that nothing *will* happen unless something new is actually put into place. "Build it and they will come," goes the mysterious line from the movie, *Field of Dreams.* As long as the one service remains, and there is no option, they cannot come, and a significant shift in the congregation's worship life is precluded. In addition, people need to be reminded that some marginal members may become active, and new members to the congregation may enter and join through the new service. The end result, therefore, will not be dividing and diminishing, but adding and growing.

In our congregation, we have three services, at three different hours, in three different locations. Though the sermon, scripture, and theme of the day are the same, the approach and worship experiences are quite different, both in content and in tone. It is true that following the addition of new worship services there is a time of "shaking out" when members of the church decide where they will worship most regularly. This may reflect a drop in attendance in one or more of the already existing services in the beginning. The question that has to be kept in mind is, "What will happen if the congregation continues to offer only one service?" The answer is usually that overall worship attendance will remain stagnant. The existing form does not provide access to many who would enter the church if they only had a meaningful doorway. If the congregation has an older median age, and is slowly declining, the trend will most likely accelerate. If that is the case, why *not* take the risk of seeing some reduction in attendance at one service if it improves the *overall* attendance at worship and attracts revitalized and new worshipers to the congregation's life?

The most threatening part of all this has to do with those who prefer traditional worship. What if, after instituting a new contemporary service, people like it more? What if all the new members start going to that service? What will happen to the service we know and love? The answers to these questions require great spiritual maturity and wisdom.

First, the focus of spiritual leadership must be on the health and well-being of the whole congregation, not one single service. Second, the wise person recognizes that just working harder at doing something in the same way and expecting different results is unrealistic.

Will we lose members over this? Will people leave? Not as many as you might think, especially if you approach it in the right way. Some loss should be anticipated in any time of change. But it is our strong feeling that more conflict will emerge over instituting a blended service than if a separate contemporary service is added while simultaneously continuing and protecting the traditional service.

The real question of faith is this: What will bring the authentic worship of God to the most people in our congregation as well as those outside our walls? Answer this question well and you are ready to move on to the next stage of actual planning.

TIME AND LOCATION

When we first began our contemporary service, we held it on Sunday evenings. Our thinking at the time was that an alternate to Sunday morning would give people more options regarding personal time and work schedules. We knew this to be true from our research into other congregations, some of which scheduled services on Sunday evening and others who elected to add a service on Saturday evening or on a weekday. The success of these options depends entirely on the nature of the congregation, its tradition, and the culture in which they are embedded. We discovered that in our particular situation, our members and visitors to our church did not view evenings as a time for regular religious observance. This, of course, is not true for many other congregations and communions that do have time-honored traditions of evening worship.

After a year of pushing forward, we realized that we had the right idea scheduled at the wrong time. We knew that a move to Sunday morning would place it squarely in the majority of both member and visitor traffic. After consultation with the elders and church leadership, it was placed right in the middle of Sunday morning between our early and late services and at the same time as our traditional church school hour. This was indeed the right choice, as evidenced by regular and increasing attendance. From that time the service became truly viable, earning its rightful place among the three services of the congregation.

The challenges for this kind of structure became immediately apparent.

First, the pastor or pastors move through the morning at the speed of light. Not only are they making large worship-style shifts as they move from one service to the next, but the time they may devote to teaching in the Christian education program is diminished. Because our congregation has two ministers, and we wanted to strengthen all of the services and give each its due attention, both attended all services. Now that the services are more clearly established, it is much easier for one of the pastors to be absent from any given service to serve in some other capacity. In the case of congregations who have one pastor, this is obviously not an option.

Second, attention must be given to families who become confused with more options. Christian education options must be created across from at least two of the services so that a family can both worship and go to a class if they so choose. Many families prefer the "one hour option" and do exactly that, generally with children in the church school while the parents worship. This has its glaring weaknesses; children lack adequate early worship experience and adults miss ongoing Christian education. The reality, however, is that these families will choose what they will choose. It is the job of the church leadership to encourage them to grow in their discipleship by participation in a small group of some sort. In any case, the multiple-option Sunday morning, for both worship and Christian education, remains the best choice for those who can achieve it.

Third, most congregations' organizational structures were created in another day and do not serve present church life adequately. When several worship services are instituted, the old structure, including all manner of lay leadership, has to be revisited and revised in order that it serves the needs of a new day. Every part belongs to a greater whole. Touch one piece and you touch everything.

Fourth, several worship options present the possibility for increased fragmentation in the congregation. This is especially true for congregations that have not yet come to see themselves as multiple-cell churches, and still understand the unity of the church as dependent on the existence of one primary gathering of the church on Sunday mornings. When our congregation added the third service, it reduced some regular opportunities for members to see one another. In addition, the attendance in several services will be somewhat reduced, at least in the early years of the model change. The ultimate goal is growth in all of the services over time.

One way we approached the need to foster more feeling of church-wide togetherness was to schedule more total congregation events. For us, this included making plans for an all-church talent show and tasting party in the spring, and then scheduling a church-wide retreat over a weekend at a retreat center in the fall. Each congregation can devise what might best foster awareness of church-wide togetherness in its own setting.

Most important, we decided to hold four "festival" Sunday mornings each year that we entitled "Come Home" Sundays. On the four Sundays of Thanksgiving, Christmas, Easter, and Pentecost we combined our three services into one large service and held it at a time dissimilar to any of our three existing services. Each of the four festival days has a special character of its own, and is accompanied by a different kind of meal. For instance, on *Come Home for Thanksgiving,* the day concludes with a traditional Thanksgiving dinner with all the trimmings. On *Come Home for Easter,* the schedule is reversed, and the morning begins with a "mega" breakfast to end all breakfasts. On *Come Home for Pentecost,* the day concludes with a barbecue held on the church lawn.

The point is that events must be intentionally scheduled to compensate for the regular lack of a whole-church experience. The experience of these events, and the resulting memory of them, reassures people that the whole church is alive and well, and that the people they have been missing are simply worshiping in another service.

Some congregations have opted for a very workable two-service, one church-school-hour model.

Christian education is sandwiched between an early service and a late service, one of which is contemporary. The pressing concern here is that many of the young families who would comprise the attenders of a contemporary service will not come to an early worship service. They desire a later hour in the morning—often the same hour where most congregations have placed traditional worship for decades! This is not insurmountable, however, and many congregations are reversing this order, with a traditional service early in the morning and the contemporary one later.

Existing congregations have limited meeting space—unless, of course, they plan to add to their building facility. As opposed to newly formed congregations, which build with more contemporary church buildings, grounds, and parking in mind from the beginning, the established congregation must make do with what has been inherited from the saints who have gone before. This can be a blessing, a curse, or a bit of both.

We are a congregation blessed with two formal worshiping spaces—a large formal sanctuary and a much smaller and more intimate chapel. This has served us very well in terms of the early morning chapel service and the later traditional service. The location of the contemporary service, however, has been more challenging. Not only are there logistical concerns about transitions, and set-up before and after services, but there also are very real aesthetic issues involving the right place for the right service.

When we moved our service to Sunday morning, we decided to hold our contemporary service in a very anti-structural locale—the church community hall. This we decorated with hangings, banners, a cross, plants, and a communion center/Lord's table in the center of the room. By careful attention to symbols and the configuration of seating, ordinary space can strangely be transformed into sacred space, especially after long periods of time during which a certain space becomes identified with the worship that takes place there.

The other side of this location issue has its merits as well. A formal sanctuary, though not naturally conducive to participatory, expressive, and informal worship events, may be adapted by placing banners on stands, moving the action off the chancel into the nave, and changing the attire of worship leaders. Most importantly, the service has the power to take over the space. Since the focus of the contemporary worship experience is on the immanent presence of God—in and among the people—rather than the transcendent presence of God, the space becomes secondary to what is actually happening to and among the gathered people of God. We have attended incredibly celebrative and innovative services in cathedral-like structures, and the space did not inhibit those worshipers in the least. Our experience has been that our community-hall setting does not necessarily detract from the power of a contemporary service. In fact, it may ironically strengthen the contemporary worship experience. The very presence of a structure already known as sacred space serves as a platform where people are given more freedom. Any transformational setting needs ritual boundaries to mediate a certain safe containment.

WHO SHALL LEAD?

However central the issues of time and location, they become mute in the absence of leadership.

As in all matters in the community of faith, spiritual leadership will determine most meaningful and lasting outcomes. This leadership must include the pastor or pastors. These challenging innovations simply will not succeed unless the pastors are at the center of the movement. Serving as more than worship leaders, they must be an integral part of the visionary team, strive to keep the whole congregation on course and united, and promote the new service both inside and outside the church. Mere consent is not sufficient, if the new contemporary service is to mean anything. Ordination most surely sets apart persons within the church for shepherd/servant leadership to the church. It is a source of authority bestowed by God through the church. But pastoral leadership is also intertwined with trust and credibility, relational dynamics that are earned over a period of tested time. And the way in which ministers exercise both this authority and influence is crucial in implementing the whole mission of the church.

Because the contemporary service, by design, resides in the *laos,* the people, and is diametrically opposed to a worship in which the institution either *presents* or *mediates* worship to participants, the leadership of the service must also reside in the people. The meaning of *liturgia,* after all, is the "work of the people." And could there be a more clearly grounded Protestant principle than the *priesthood of all believers?*

It is close to the hearts of many religious movements, certainly among heirs of the Stone-Campbell movement—i.e., the Christian Church (Disciples of Christ). This suggests an approach to leadership that is perfectly suited for our present culture, a culture not only suspicious of hierarchy but also unwilling to be a part of systems dominated by it. Leadership, including that of the ordained, will increasingly emerge collaboratively from *within* and not from *above*.

As the idea of contemporary worship grows and the word gets out, you will discover interesting people surfacing. Some of them will come from the center of present church life. More often than not, these new key leaders and servants will appear from the "edges," the experimental, innovative margins where most change usually occurs. This means that the marginally active, or inactive, will step forward when they find something that excites their spiritual longings. They are ready to serve, and with encouragement and guidance will provide some of your most important leadership. New persons to a congregation frequently feel most comfortable pitching in on something new that is still fluid and with boundaries not yet set in stone. This is true as one considers creating new classes or groups for Christian education. An established group already has unwritten membership lists and perimeters. New classes are still open, not only to including new persons but also in the way they allow and encourage those persons to help shape the future.

If this is true for small groups within the church, it is doubly true for leadership within an emerging contemporary service. In other words, there is still room for new persons to offer their spiritual gifts, practice a meaningful stewardship, and become part of the leadership of a new worshiping community within the congregation.

This leadership includes planning, suggesting, and implementing changes, serving in ways that actually make the service happen, and leading in worship. And the key to organizing this leadership has to do with a team approach.

THE ROUNDTABLE TEAM MODEL

The way to create this leadership of the people is to conceptualize your leadership groups in terms of teams gathered around a common round table. The theological significance of this model should not be lost on us!

Each team has a focused set of priorities for its ministry and a key person or persons who are the contact or coordinator for that team. The size of each team depends on the needs of the congregation and the purpose of the team. In our congregation, we gather around the table this way:

Set-Up Team: This team takes care of logistical concerns such as setting up chairs, sound equipment, offering, communion, attendance pads, flowers, and banners. Their mission is to prepare the physical space for the worship experience. We use a rotation in which team members take one Sunday each month.

Put-Away Team: They undo everything the set-up team put up at the end of the service. In our church, this team includes one particular family and any friends who will help!

Reach-Out Team: Their mission is to set up the name-tag board, put out promotional materials, greet attenders, and make special contact with new visitors in our midst. We also use a rotation of team members for this ministry.

Music Team: This team takes the theme of the day and designs a musical approach that enhances and embodies it. They are responsible, in consultation with the pastor, for everything having to do with musical leadership within the service. This team is a set group of eight musicians.

Worship Leadership Team: A rotation of worship leaders provides actual leadership in the worship services. In our congregation these leaders read the scripture lessons and lead the time of prayer. The pastors most usually preach and officiate at the Lord's table.

Pastoral Team: The ministers work together in coordinating the service with the season of the year, selecting theme/scripture of the day, keeping the teams moving in the same direction, and acting as resident theologians.

Though most of the actual work of these teams is done fairly independently, with each team concentrating on its own particular ministry, it is important periodically to gather the teams around the common table for a roundtable summit. We have called summits when we are moving into a new season and need to communicate more clearly about our shared ministries. We also have roundtable summits when we are either evaluating our ministry or deliberating on matters that will affect the whole service. Anyone can suggest the need for a summit, but in practice this task usually falls to the pastors. These occasions have served as important moments in our lives together as we seek a common mind and vision in the spirit.

This roundtable of teams relates to the rest of the congregation and its organizational structures, especially through such existing entities as the worship committee. The key to a vibrant and energetic new worship community, however, is its self-sufficiency. By that, we do not mean an independence from the rest of the congregation—that would encourage fragmentation. Rather, we mean the responsibility participants must take for their own service. This differs sharply from former models of church life in which the institution takes care of a service by design; certain people serve by virtue of some assigned post in the church. By contrast, the roundtable of teams model asks participants to take responsibility for their own worship life. This kind of investment and participation by the people contribute to the sense of purpose and the warmth of Christian community.

*T*he only thing worse than idolizing *form* to the extent that it is revered more than the substance it attempts to convey is to idolize the *change* of form to the detriment of substance. What is found in the worst-case scenarios of contemporary worship innovation is a kind of shallow, frothy, emotion-only driven worship that has sacrificed all theological integrity. Sunday morning *lite*. The kind of place where you leave hungry.

For example, we have visited churches where the act of baptism is haphazard, if not comical. In other worship settings we discovered an attempt to reach out to the so-called "seekers" to such a degree that the sacraments were either not thoughtfully considered in a new context or were intentionally hidden altogether. As visitors, we read in one worship bulletin that all those interested in baptism were invited to come to the church on Wednesday evening at 6:30 p.m. to view the "baptism video," to be followed by baptisms at 7:30 p.m.! In the same congregation, the Lord's supper was celebrated monthly at a midweek service in order not to confuse seekers on Sunday. The pastor invited the people to attend in these seeker-sensitive words: "You know, a long time ago, Jesus had a meal

Somebody Has to Be the Theologian!

with his friends, and it was really special. We have the same kind of thing, and Jesus would really appreciate it if you would come...." We are sure he did.

At its worst, we have found the preaching of the astonishing and shocking gospel reduced to a list of religious-sounding helpful hints for positive living, with verses of scripture snatched from here and there to prove a point. The morass of music in much of the contemporary worship scene is like flypaper dragged through a sandpile—an eclectic and often contradictory gathering of theological and philosophical bits and pieces.

Who shall save us from this body of death? Thanks be to God, it is your friendly neighborhood theologian!

It is the pastor who must first serve in the role of resident theologian. This means the pastor has both the authority and responsibility to reflect theologically on all aspects of the service, from the identified themes to the practice of the sacraments. In this way, the pastor is serving as teacher of the community. When initiating new form, *didache,* which means "teaching," becomes increasingly important. At its best, this is done collaboratively, drawing in the leadership of the service as they become a part of a community of theological reflection.

Why is it that we do what we do? Does this new idea fit with the rest of what we do, and why? Is this particular music or hymnody appropriate, and for what reason? The way the community both asks and answers these kinds of questions will determine the kinds of decisions that are made and, in the end, the kind of service that shall become.

SOURCES OF AUTHORITY

If we were to take John Wesley's four sources of authority, his quadrilateral, and use them together as a model for evaluating contemporary worship, how would we do so? If the sources of authority in the church may be identified as *scripture, tradition, reason,* and *experience,* how might reflection on these separate but related aspects inform the worshiping community?

First, a community of theological reflection will listen to the word of *scripture* as it points us to our highest authority, God. As a library of witnesses, the scripture speaks to our present-day community of believers as we attempt to discern the ancient wisdom for this present day. We must interpret the scripture with all of the tools and spirit at our disposal. This interpretation must not be limited to the domain of the pastor in sermon preparation; it is the very rock on which the entire house must stand. The words of scripture lead us to the revealed Word of God, Jesus Christ, who remains the life-giving presence in our midst and host of our communion table.

Are the themes that guide our worship service grounded in the biblical story, clearly reflecting the Christian message?

Does the pastor's message clearly exegete the text and bring a word of faith to the church in this present moment?

Do the components that make up the service have biblical mooring, as reflected in the core New Testament practices of the church such as preaching, teaching, praying, praising, baptizing, caring for the weakest among us, and breaking the bread?

Is the hymnody consistent with the way the community interprets its scripture in the rest of its life?

Second, a community of theological reflection will listen to the voices from its own and the larger Christian *tradition.*

We live within the continuity of the communion of the saints. That is to say, a cloud of witnesses surrounds us not only spatially but temporally. We share the faith with communities of faith spanning the centuries. We are heirs of the ways in which the Christian communities have worshiped throughout time.

The Reformed tradition reminds us that the church is reformed, yet always reforming. Part of this understanding is that we are to maintain a lively conversation with our own tradition. This lively conversation listens to the wealth of riches in our tradition, which has shaped us in many ways. It also is willing to challenge the presuppositions of any one tradition if they are not consistent with other sources of authority, such as scripture.

In our own worship tradition from the Christian Church (Disciples of Christ), we have received the gifts of the proclaimed word balanced with the every-Sunday table,[+] the heart-felt faith living alongside rational

---

[+] For the Disciples of Christ, the Lord's supper is the central and indispensable act of worship that we share in every worship service. This reclaiming of the centrality of the Lord's table came in our search for the normative essentials of worship as found in the New Testament, and it is one of our communion's gifts to the ecumenical church. As more denominations are rediscovering the table as a result of their enlarged ecumenical life, contemporary worship provides yet another opportunity for Protestants to reclaim the eucharist as the center of the church's worship life.

inquiry, a wealth of hymnody derived primarily from the nineteenth and early-twentieth centuries, and the understanding and practice of strong lay leadership. Much of our tradition we inherited from other traditions. To that, we added our distinctive turns of interpretation and re-formation. That receiving and re-forming made us into the distinctive body that we are within the larger body of Christ. As local congregations and their cultures have varied according to theology, context, and practice, worship forms among particular congregations have also been unique; each congregation also has *its* tradition. Because of this kind of historical development, everything we are and do comes first from somewhere else. We must view ourselves as connected in this powerful way, not unrelated to the spiritual domains from whence we have come.

As interpreters of our congregation's tradition, we respect the gifts it brings to us. As those who are reformed, yet always reforming, we are not hesitant to build on those traditions in new and different ways, attempting to remain faithful to the principles that have guided us. In a time when we have come to understand the relative nature of cultures and how they have manifested themselves within the church, we also claim as our own the worshiping traditions of our brothers and sisters, both near and far, which are quite different than our own. Though we claim them, we do not attempt to copy them. Instead, we appropriate into our own worship the rich textures they have given to the larger church, insofar as they are consistent with our understanding of the faith.

As a by-product of the ecumenical movement of this century, Christians are becoming aware of how our particular theological and worship traditions reside within the larger context of the one, holy, and apostolic church of Jesus Christ. The unity we seek embraces Christian tradition throughout time, among different communal families within the whole Christian household, and increasingly the church as found in a many-textured, multicultural international context. The *oikomene,* the whole inhabited world, is the province of God, and it is filled with the *evangelion,* the good news of Jesus Christ. The *ekklesia,* the glad people of God, celebrate the redeeming, saving, liberating power of the Spirit as the whole creation continues to be filled with the glory of God's presence.

Such an awareness of the one Lord, one faith, and one baptism of the one church in which we stand can be reflected in a joyful worship. The fresh indigenous Christian hymnody from Africa or Latin America, the haunting lyrics from the British Isles, or the contemplative chants from such communities as Taize all open enriched and reconciling windows to a people tempted to remain provincial, isolated, or self-preoccupied.

Third, a community of theological reflection will utilize the capacity for *reason* in the quest for a thoughtful faith.

If Christians understand that, as one early church father put it, the whole theological enterprise is *faith seeking understanding,* we will bring all capacities of mind, rationality, and reason to our faith. If the grace of faith is a gift of God, the capacity for its reception and our perception is also a gift. Though human understanding is finite and limited, we seek to understand to the fullest measure of our capacity, with the guidance of the spirit which enlightens, inspires, and sanctifies.

As Christians seek to bring a clear word to a contemporary world that is knowingly or unknowingly starving for its Creator, they do what the church has always needed to do: they engage in the classical discipline of *apologetics*. From the church fathers of the first few centuries, the high philosophical theology of medieval scholasticism, the reformers of the sixteenth century, the liberal enterprise of the nineteenth century, the Social Gospel movement of early twentieth century, the method of correlation, process thought and theological reflection, or the liberation theologies grappling with the gospel for the most oppressed, the church has always attempted to make sense of the faith for its own time and context and engaged its receptive or skeptical audiences in persuasive or understandable terms.

In the social and religious contexts of late-twentieth century North America, people are daring the church to speak a meaningful and relevant word. Why is it that our supposedly religiously indifferent culture so fills its news magazines and television with things religious? However trite the fare may be, this betrays an underlying hunger for transcendence and spiritual depth. And if the church cannot or will not engage this culture at the point of this need, it will simply turn elsewhere.

People who come to our churches today want a faith that makes sense to them. Their lives are confusing. The world and society around them is fragmented. Families are under unprecedented stress. The world of work is in flux. Change is coming at the speed of light in massive quantity. In addition, the implicit moorings of broadly accepted faith in the culture is absent. If people are going to find any faith claims of substance, they will come from the church and not automatically from the culture. What these people need is the radical, counter-cultural option. And it must have intellectual integrity in order to be heard in the midst of many other competing voices.

The message of the amazing love of God, revealed in the Christ, the power that reconciles God to humanity and humanity to itself, is sheer power! The self-conscious celebration of this reality in worship brings the liberating word to those living in bondage. It engenders Christian growth. It empowers Christian service. The multifaceted Gospel is sufficient to bring rest to the weary and heavy-laden. The people of God provide a community that is large enough to hold the loneliness. The challenge is so pointed that we cannot stay where we are. Resurrection people are new creatures.

Our messages, our music, our praising, and our prayer must engage the lives of those who gather with us. To make contact, we must not compromise our message in some attempt to reduce it to the lowest common denominator. We rather need to *translate* it in understandable terms. This means reaching out to where they live and breathe...but not stopping there.

That is only the beginning point of contact. It means going higher, painting a picture of the *baseleia,* the reign of God that is and will be. The true gift to the person seeking a reasonable faith is not only something that sounds familiar, but is also something that is *more* than the familiar. Why else would I come to you looking for the bread of life? If you are simply going to dish out more of the same fare I am served every other day from my ordinary world, why would I bother to come to you? Don't just hold up a mirror to my face. I want more than I am and what I am presently seeing. Why else would I stay or commit? I get that every day everywhere else. Give me more. Give me a larger vision. Let me feast on the riches of Christ. But please, put it in terms *I can understand.*

Fourth, a community of theological reflection will claim *experience* as a gateway to the working of God in our midst.

Of all the things that might motivate persons to come to our churches in the first place, it is frequently a longing for religious experience that is most predominant. Though this varies from person to person, from generation to generation, and from one culture to another, this desire for an experiential encounter with God often plays a determining role in the religious affiliations that are chosen.

A dry and lifeless atmosphere is death to those seeking a faith that meets them at the point of their human need. This is one of the reasons that communities of the spirit, both in the American neo-Pentecostal form and in movements all over the world found primarily in the southern hemisphere, find themselves growing. Whether the theology is progressive, fundamentalist, or something in-between, the movements that accentuate the personal experience of the sacred are reaching out to ever-larger numbers of hungry searchers.

This experiential dimension of faith, this direct encounter with God for the individual and within the community, is at the heart of contemporary worship. Whether it be contemplative in form or profoundly expressive, the faith has to make contact, and it has to make contact on a very basic, emotional level. It is not sufficient to talk *about* a relationship with God; the relationship must *actually occur in the present moment.* Our prayer should not be composed of tomes about God but should give humble address *to* a living and loving God.

Worship must offer an antidote to the alienation, one-dimensionality, noisy meaninglessness, and quiet desperation of our time. This includes a tangible sense of close Christian community, an apprehension of awe and wonder, a stillness or quietude, and most of all, the joy of the spirit. Unless religious communities can offer these things, and do so in their worship, they simply will not make contact with the contemporary soul.

The strength of the experiential basis of religious knowledge, subjectivity, is also its weakness and danger. For instance, my experience and your experience may lead us to quite different conclusions. My personal experience may lead me to distorted, unrealistic, or destructive choices. For instance, Jim Jones (of Jonestown infamy) had a community of religious experience, as has every religious cult that has ever placed dramatic claims upon its adherents, but the experience did not lead to a healthy community. It is no wonder that Alexander Campbell, one of the founders of the Christian Church (Disciples of Christ), was so profoundly suspicious of the raw emotion found in much of the frontier revival movement. Unattached to an anchor beyond itself, experience alone is not a sufficient ground for a solid and lasting faith. And if the atmosphere and context of contemporary worship is determined by a strong experiential component, which it certainly needs, it becomes even more important to keep it standing upon the foundations of scripture, tradition, and reason. In this way, experience is tempered by a larger frame of reference against which it always needs to be measured.

Yes, someone has to be the ongoing theologian for contemporary worship to maintain its integrity and honor its most important core mission. Then, and only then, will it be prepared to reach out to a whole new generation of people hungry for the gospel.

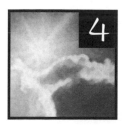

4

Much has been written and presented about evangelism toward those who are either not Christian or not active Christians who take part in a worshiping body. Most of these same evangelism and church-growth principles apply to contemporary worship settings. In fact, contemporary worship itself serves as a primary evangelism initiative in the congregation.

When we first began our contemporary service, we planned many special emphasis Sundays and promoted the service in special ways in order to attract people to it. Part of this was necessary because we needed to strengthen the identity of a new service. We always appreciated the patience of our members who worshiped in other services that were *not* receiving the same kind of promotion. In time, individual promotion of the service diminished when the primary means of getting the word out became the invitation given by participants to their friends and acquaintances.

More importantly, the service eventually became a full member of the totality of worship opportunities offered by the whole congregation. This became a very attractive part of a whole program that we offered to prospective and new members. We came to explain the Sunday morning experience as a whole, with contemporary worship being one of those options.

35

WOULD YOU TRANSLATE THAT, PLEASE?

We believe that the Christian message must be heard clearly for a new day. In order to be heard, it must be spoken in a recognizable language. And we need to keep two things in mind.

First, the message ought not be watered down to a lowest common denominator, a kind of floating, pseudo-spiritual thing that is intertwined with the most prevalent ideology or trendy psychology so that it is easily sold. The integrity of Christian life is lost.

Second, the message *does* indeed need to be translated, and translated in several ways. It needs to be translated into the present *context* in which people find themselves living. If the Gospel is *incarnational*, it has to enter my actual human life and existence and matter.

Language is a repository of symbol and meaning. As such, it both shapes and is shaped by thought. The language of worship carries with it specific meanings which, when altered, are changed if not lost. And here is the rub: *Some of the codified language of the church is not discernible by contemporary unchurched persons.* They need to have a translation made and put into the vernacular. Christians leading worship need to be aware of the need for this translation for the sake of the hearer. But they also must be aware of what is *lost* in the translation. For example, using potato chips and soda pop for communion destroys the symbol-laden sharing of bread and wine. You have indeed translated into a popular idiom, but you have also lost the original meaning in the translation.

In addition, some of the language of the church exists not so much because it is central to the gospel but because it has accommodated to the culture at a particular point in time. This language may be archaic and may reflect roles, a worldview, and ways of understanding Christian discipleship that are time-bound. Separating what is essential from what is non-essential is the primary task of contemporary worship leadership!

We have approached this dilemma in several ways. First, we have replaced archaic language that we assess as non-essential with familiar language used in the present culture. An example might be the terms we use to describe the different components of worship. Instead of using *The Act of Fellowship*, you could describe this movement of the service as *The Gathering of the People.* The *Sermon* could instead be listed as *Sharing the Good News.* The *Benediction* could become *The Sending Out.*

It goes without saying that hymnody stands at the center of this issue. A good argument can be made that, after the Bible, the hymnals of any tradition have held the most formative influence in the shaping of Christians in the life of faith. Unfortunately, much of the hymnody that has been central to most traditions falls on ears which do not *hear* it. This has to do with its archaic language, musical style from another era, and instruments that are used to accompany the congregation's singing. For those of us who grew up in the church, this usually presents no obstacle. In fact, the familiarity of words, tunes, and instrumentation brings back a flood of rich memory affiliations.

But for those who are unchurched, who have not shared that same experience or been a part of that churchly culture, it presents a strange combination of sounds and ideas.

One of the gifts to the church has been continuing new hymnody that uses current musical idiom, present forms of language, and poignant language that speaks more clearly to the contemporary person. Some of our finest new hymnals blend much of the best traditional hymnody with this new wealth of the church's song.

In terms of evangelism and reaching out to spiritual guests in our midst, a new language of worship that both makes contact *and* has integrity opens doors for those who really *do* want to hear a word of life.

Secondly, there are certain components of worship we have defined as essential, and we are unwilling to abandon them. They remain present and virtually unchanged, though perhaps in simple form. Not only are they theologically indispensable, but they also provide the necessary structure to offset the relative freedom of contemporary worship. People need structure, even of a minimalist degree, in order to express their deepest feelings. For all of the seeming chaos, sporting events, rock concerts, and even impressionistic videos contain more implicit structure and dramatic narrative than meets the eye. And if there is not some degree of structure, the anxiety level of participants—especially new participants—is simply too high for comfort. It is not safe enough!

As opposed to some wings of the contemporary worship movement, we do not play down unique and essential aspects of worship, such as the sacraments. *We play them up!* In our tradition, the Lord's supper stands at the center of worship in every gathering of the people of God. The fact that we are worshiping in a contemporary form does not change that. In fact, it becomes increasingly important that we *do* have it. The way that we celebrate the supper may be simple, but the essentials are present. The same is true of baptism. When we have the opportunity to celebrate Christian baptism, we do not hide it, we *expose* it. We make it an event central to the worshiping community.

How does this relate to evangelism? We attempt to let powerful, universal symbols speak. And instead of hiding or concealing them, we explain and teach about them. Don't remove the unfamiliar but powerful; introduce it!

> *I have not come to your spiritual home looking for what I see all the time on the outside. I expect to find something different. Don't apologize to me for having it. Instead, share it with me, translate it for me.*

BE INTENTIONAL

So you both expect new visitors and want them to become connected to your community of faith? That's good. But it won't happen unless you are intentional about it.

Of the many things a congregation may do to be evangelistically intentional, we have focused on at least six in our contemporary worship:

1. Information Boards at the Entrances. These boards are mounted on the walls and have pockets that contain information about the church. There are descriptions of the various worship services, Christian education opportunities, and a map of the building. Not only do visitors take the material on their own, but it provides a natural point of discussion as members may simply take them to the info board and say, "Here is some information that may be helpful to you...."

2. Greeters Providing Name Tags. Every Sunday we have a team of greeters at the back of the gathering space who individually greet those who attend, with a special eye to meeting new persons in our midst. A name tag board is present, and the greeters make new name tags for new people. In addition, information about the church and upcoming programs is found on the name tag table.

3. Recognizing the Guests. Some people and congregations are hesitant about singling out new persons in their midst to publicly recognize them. That is a choice you will have to make. We have decided to simply ask for those who are first-time visitors to raise their hands. The servers bring them a simple gift, and we thank them for attending. This also enables members to introduce themselves during or at the close of the service.

4. Encouraging Gregarious Mixing at a Welcome Time. After an opening time of singing, we have a time of free mixing when we invite people to greet one another. It is not nearly as formal as a liturgical passing of the peace. It is pandemonium. And we encourage it, and it goes on for a while! This allows for both building a sense of togetherness, which is one of the very reasons people have come to visit, and also gives members the opportunity to greet new visitors.

5. Follow-up with First-time Visitors. As a part of church-wide evangelism, a contact ministry calls on all first-time visitors with a "screen door" call on the Sunday afternoon of their first visit. They come bringing information about the church and a freshly baked treat, like cookies. A report is carried back to the contact ministry coordinator, who tracks the future attendance of these visitors and contacts them.

6. Encouraging Our Members to Invite Friends and Acquaintances. The hardest thing about evangelism is overcoming the reluctance of people to share their faith and enthusiasm about their church with others. This fear of uncomfortableness is understandable. In a highly individualistic and privatistic culture, people feel as though such actions are imposing. And yet, this is the single most effective way to reach out. It is an ongoing aspect of our Christian education!

$\mathcal{J}$f the context of much modern life is that of isolation and loneliness, the answer of the gospel is the biblical concept of *koinonia*. This spirit-based sense of community and belonging is different than any other because its basis is not like-mindedness or homogeneity. Its source is a common life in Christ. As such, it is different than other forms of association of like-minded people, whose connection is limited to shared activities and ceases when those activities cease to hold importance. Koinonia, on the other hand, is a gift received as one is initiated into the body of Christ through baptism. It is the centrality of Christ in our community that creates community and engenders the unity of the church for which Christ prayed.

The sharing of worship among the people of God creates a strong sense of Christian community. And the movements within worship and the connections coming from worship either build it up or tear it down. In addition to the ways the foundation stones of Christian worship create community, which we will address later, there are several ways in which congregations may foster a growing sense of deep Christian relationship.

GATHERING TIME

As opposed to formal or traditional worship, where the accent is generally on the transcendence of God, and attention moving from pew to altar, contemporary worship stresses the immanence of God with the Presence centered in the midst of the people. This means that the Spirit is among those who are gathered, and the open relating and sharing of worshipers together is not an appendage to worship, like a warm-up, *but part of worship itself.* For this reason, introverts and thinkers sometimes find the open interaction and feeling among worshipers in contemporary worship uncomfortable.

We remember our first visit to a large, African-American, Roman Catholic Church that was contemporary in its worship form. At the sharing of the peace, absolute pandemonium broke loose. The capacity crowd began milling about and talking and greeting one another. One of our parents visiting with us remarked, "Is the service over?" No, the service was not over…it was just beginning. This greeting and milling continued for at least fifteen minutes. The magic of Christian community was spilling into the aisles.

When we began our contemporary service, we built in community gathering time as an intentional part of the service from the very beginning. At first, people may have been hesitant, but not for long. Now the community gathering time, which we have after singing together for ten or fifteen minutes, goes on for some time—and we have to ask them to come back to their seats! This gathering time has now become an expected and indispensable part of our worship, and it contributes to the warm and interactive sense of our service. To the first-time observer, it may seem to be random chaos. Perhaps it is! But this chaos is regulated by an underlying powerful force, one that also creates Christian community, and that is the power of ritual.

THE RITUAL-MAKERS

One of the assumptions made about contemporary worship is that it is devoid of structure. That might be an easy conclusion to draw, for the movement away from traditional worship has often meant a departure from both its structure and order. What we have found, however, is exactly the opposite.

One of our great surprises has been just how important structure is to those who are innovating and creating the new. There is a deep need in the human psyche for repetitive, predictable form to offset freedom. Just as jazz improvisation depends upon an underlying rhythmic and harmonic structure, so free forms of worship need simple structure. This need is often manifested in the creation and continuing of collective rituals which mediate order, meaning, and diversity in a community. Observation of a worshiping community for any period of time will reveal an implicit, if unwritten, structure of worship.

Our canon of collective rituals developed fairly quickly. The order of the service, however simple, became ritualized. Certain expected aspects became treasured and missed if absent. Our canon of rituals became our gathering time, a time of mutual sharing of joys and concerns in conjunction with our prayer time, the Lord's Prayer, and the Lord's table.

The highest and most significant of the ritual actions is the sharing of the Lord's supper. The physical table sits in the center of the worship area, with the community literally wrapped around and facing the table. It is always set with colors of the season, bread, wine, and a candle. It is the meditative focal point of what would otherwise be just a very simply decorated room. The method of distribution is a common loaf and cup, by intinction. This act of coming forward to the table up a common aisle as we sing, dipping the bread into the cup and returning to seats, has become a powerful and expected ritual. This form of communing has brought a balance of transcendence and immanence to our midst. We go forward together and share the riches of Christ from the same loaf and cup. It is not only that the supper must happen—for in our tradition the table is central in all worship—but the *ritualized way* that the people commune has now become a part of the way we share our lives together.

As symbols are not created, but instead emerge from the universal depths of a community's life in God, so community-forming rituals are not arbitrarily fabricated. Wise leaders must use great discernment as they watch the life of a community evolve and notice the deep patterns that the community is repeating, claiming, and owning. In time, these rituals both define and reinforce Christian community, if not in visible form, then at least by their underlying structure.

CONNECTING THROUGH SMALL GROUPS

The genius of the Sunday school movement was that congregations would grow by cellular formation. The whole was strengthened by the parts. However important the ministry of teaching, one of the primary results of the adult Sunday school was the formation of a close-knit Christian community. Life-long friendships were formed and still exist in the Sunday school classes existing in our churches today. And the synergy of these places of nurture provided the fellowship core of the congregation.

Times have changed. Sunday school is no longer the entry point for church participation, as it often was in the 1940s and 1950s. The entry point today is worship for adults and Sunday school for children. A smaller percentage of our members participate in Sunday school classes and men's and women's groups. Christian community is diminished by this, but the old paradigm will no longer serve us. What will?

We now have to begin with worship as the primary gathering place, and then spin off small groups from this larger body. The movement is from the whole to its parts. The task is to create an array of small-group options that complement the time of worship. These options may be long-term commitments, but today will just as often be short-term opportunities—somewhere between four and eight weeks in length. People are more willing to make short-term commitments to a subject matter that directly addresses their spiritual growth.

The contemporary worship service becomes the link to these other options, and participants are urged to attend within the service itself. This is most effective when leadership comes from their own members—one of them—and provides a personal invitation. Class sessions need to vary according to a plurality of spiritual development. For those who are new to the Christian journey, a class on Christian basics can be most helpful. But for those who have gone deeper, classes such as *Christians Face the Tough Questions* or *Tapping a Living Spirituality* will make more meaningful contact.

In addition to classes, ongoing support groups and, more directly, recreational groups may augment and enrich the community's shared life.

Churches that have adopted a meta model for church life conceptualize the church as comprised of a primary worshiping body surrounded by multiple *cells* or family groups. These discipleship groups serve as the primary place of Christian growth, accountability, community, and service. Linked to the main worshiping body, they provide the intimacy a larger inspirational gathering cannot.

However congregations address this need, we must find ways to provide meaningful small-group life that is directly tied to the contemporary service. Because the whole is always greater than the sum of its parts, worship will be strengthened because of it. Because intimacy derives in large part from small-group experience, participants will find a sense of close Christian community in a fragmented and alienated world.

During the past year, a Christian man from Egypt was visiting our city as a guest of the World Student Christian Federation. He attended a contemporary service, and though his tradition was Coptic Orthodoxy—and he was therefore unfamiliar with our style of worship as well as our music—he later reflected, "It is impossible for me to explain, but I sensed the Spirit as part of a family, a spirit of joy and warmth, a presence of the Lord in the room. I could feel it." Later he asked us, "Are you all family?" We knew what he meant. His question came from his own experience of families and extended families making up local worship communities in his own country. But such was not the case in the sense he meant. Very few of us are tied by blood. But we are joined together by something the genetics cannot offer. It is the *koinonia*, the Spirit-filled community of the body of Christ.

$\mathcal{Y}$ou have determined just why it is that you want to launch into an alternative, contemporary form of worship. Instead of starting prematurely, a forming leadership team has prepared the congregation and sought its support. In preparation for a new service, measures have been taken to assess the impact on the whole morning, including Christian education. Time and location have been determined, and leadership teams have been appointed to handle all of the logistics of worship. You even have plans in place at least to start some small-group and Christian education tie-ins to the new service. But now your first Sunday is upon you. What will it actually look like? What will be its shape and content? How much form and how little? In what order should the movements of worship take place? You feel some tension along the back of your shoulders, and your stomach has butterflies. Are you ready?

A MINISTRY OF WORD AND SACRAMENT

Relax. Remember that it's not your job to recreate the *essentials*. Just because you are using a contemporary form does not mean that you have jettisoned your tradition. As a part of the universal, holy, and apostolic church of the centuries, and as heirs of your particular religious heritage, you remain a community grounded in *word* and *sacrament.* That means you will still be incorporating the riches of the proclamation and the great thanksgiving of God's people at the table of the Lord. Whatever else happens, these two poles will ground your experience with theological integrity and connect you to the ecumenical church.

The implementation may be different, but the essence will remain constant. These two powers must be broken open for the worshiping community. Whether the Lord's table is a part of this pattern every week depends on each church's approach to the sacraments. But regardless of frequency, the balance between word and table remains.

First, you break open the good news of Christ, the Word of God, as found in the scriptures. Secondly, you break the bread and pour the wine—the great feast of remembrance, Christ's real presence, the future hope, the ultimate sign of the unity of the church. And in these twin acts, the transcendent dimension will come to a hungry people all too familiar with and jaded by one-dimensional living. They need the mystery from beyond, or else they wouldn't have bothered to come in the first place. Don't dish out what they get every day in the world. It's not worth serving. However the message is communicated or the table is spread, you must trust that the word and sacrament will provide living water that is a spring gushing up to eternal life.

THE FLOW OF THE SERVICE

A worship service takes place in time and space. The space part you have figured out. But what about time? What shall be the sequence of the community's acts of worship? Shall you use the traditional shape of the liturgy, or just dump the pieces out on the table and put them together in some sensible order? How do you decide?

As the shape of the liturgy has developed historically and yielded widely different forms, we know that there is no one absolute order for the act of worship. We do, however, have guidance from our own traditions and the larger ecumenical community of worship of which we are a part. We know from the testimony of scripture and tradition which component parts of worship are normative. And we place them in an order that makes theological sense and provides dramatic ritual movement.

We want an order of service that fosters a sense of movement, flow, and direction. Because worship is primarily a transformative experience that takes place in a sacred and set-apart time and space, there must be a clear sense of entrance, transition, and conclusion to complete the process. And in contemporary forms of worship, simplicity is the key to understanding the form that enables a transforming worship passage to occur.

THE WORSHIP PATTERN

Our congregation uses an order of service that proceeds from praise and community-building to the engagement with the Word, to the deepening of prayer, to the mystery of the sacrament of the Lord's supper, and finally a sending forth. Though this order was not carved into tablets on top of the mount, we find that it moves the congregation through a process that leads them more and more deeply toward a transformational relationship with God. (See Appendix One for a summary of this pattern.)

PRAISE

As psalms of praise opened the worship of the synagogue, and later the early church, so we begin our contemporary worship with a time of joyful and uplifting doxology. The goal of this singing is to lift the heart toward God in praise and adoration. We customarily sing three or four songs, for a period of ten to fifteen minutes, and the songs reflect the glory, majesty, and greatness of God and confess our need for and trust in God. This is the beginning movement of worship for a community full of the joy of God. And in a time flush with anxiety, depression, and emptiness, what better place to begin than with turning the heart toward what is truly worthy of our praise.

This opening section also includes songs of the season and songs related to the theme of the day. In the season of Advent we might sing a new setting of the *Magnificat*, or in Christmas a lively setting of *Gloria in Excelsis Deo* in the form of a round. If the theme has to do with taking the Christmas joy out of the stable into the world, the congregation might sing *Go Tell It On the Mountain.* In any case, we keep the more uplifting hymnody that inspires awe, community, and joy in this first section of the service. The more somber, meditative, or confessional material we schedule later, often in close proximity to prayer. (See the following chapter for an overview of music in contemporary worship.)

THE RITUAL OF COMMUNITY

Immediately following the initial singing, the congregation is asked to greet all of those around them, "especially those new in our midst, or people you have not met." At this point, leadership communicates an expectation that this time of greeting is to go on for some time. The ministers and band members leave the front of the worship area and physically go out into the gathered people, lingering, and talking in an unhurried way. You want this to go on for some time! Your goal is to have to *ask* them to stop when it looks like they *never* will.

Immediately after reconvening the body, we ask our first-time visitors to raise their hands and introduce themselves. At this time our servers give them a simple welcome gift and the congregation extends our greeting to them by applauding their presence. This gathering time is concluded by sharing news and announcements of the church community.

The Worship Experience

THE SERVICE OF THE WORD

The scripture lesson is chosen in conjunction with the theme of the morning and the message of the sermon. In turn, the music and corresponding prayers and meditations often reflect this scripturally-based theme. A layperson reads the lesson, which is immediately followed by the message.

The message is presented by one of the ministers who relates the core theme(s) of the lesson to the life of faith. Though a full reflection on preaching in contemporary worship is outside the purview of this book, and it has received expanded attention in other publications, we would like to offer a few suggestions:

• Dress casually. Vestments are out, but dressy attire communicates seriousness. Use your own good judgment, because much of this depends on the social setting in which your church is placed. The goal is to remove barriers between speaker and receiver. To give you an idea, in our congregation the male ministers wear shirt sleeves and ties and female ministers wear dresses or suits.

• Simplify, but don't "dumb-down." You want a sermon message that is as clear as a bell. But simple does not equal simplistic. Be deep, but apparent. Go ahead and talk about eschatology, but put it in terms people understand—for instance, "God's future and the horizon of hope." At the end of the message, anyone should be able to answer the following question with a single sentence: "What was the sermon about?"

• Use narrative preaching when appropriate, and always use plenty of *relevant* stories and illustrations. As one of my good friends has said, "You've got to turn theology into biography." It's true. Unless it becomes biographical, the theological is often not accessed. Bring the idea home. Apply the following criteria as you consider using any illustration: (1) Does it cause me to say, "Aha!"? (2) Does it cause me to exclaim, "What?" (3) Does it bring me to tears? or (4) Does it bring me to laughter?

• Get out from behind the lectern or pulpit. You may feel shy and exposed at first, but you can't hide forever. No, you can't stand behind the decorative plant either. If you move from behind the lectern, remember that people cannot easily follow a moving target. Though some preachers like to pace, and often do so out of their own anxiety, resist the temptation to become a homiletical ping-pong ball!

• Don't preach from a manuscript—your ideas should be simple enough and you should be familiar enough with your message that you only need notes. At best, don't use notes either. Change the location of your communication from a space somewhere between speaker and notes, to a space somewhere between speaker and listener.

• Communication is largely non-verbal. If you want the message to get through, speak with passion and feeling, preach only what you truly believe, use your voice and your body for accent and emphasis, and dare to be a servant conduit between the Gospel and the actual lives before you.

If the pastor must preach in more than one worship service on a Sunday morning, the same scripture basis and message may be used in all settings. The difference between sermons in these different services is primarily a stylistic one. Though content may be omitted, adjusted, or added in light of the service in which one is preaching, the manner of delivery will necessarily change. The contemporary service will demand a more extemporaneous, immediate, conversational form of communication. And an important by-product of developing a compelling delivery in the context of contemporary worship is the renewal of preaching in all areas. The principles of communication that make for effective preaching in the contemporary setting no doubt enliven preaching in the more formal, traditional worship service. Pastor and people alike may expect new dimensions of proclamation to emerge.

PRAYER

The prayer of the people is at the heart of the gathered community, and collective or corporate prayer is distinct from individual prayer. This prayer is an act of the entire community. To set this prayer time squarely in the life of the people, we open our prayer with a time for sharing prayer concerns and joys. This may embrace the most personal of concerns, such as the illness of family members, as well as global concerns involving Christian compassion and response. You may be surprised at the depth and emotion of the concerns that are shared. On occasion this time of sharing may continue for quite some time. The openness of members to share personal and sometimes intimate issues is directly related to the degree of acceptance and trust within the community. Most generally, the prayer leader, who may be either lay or clergy, makes a note of these concerns as they are shared, and then incorporates them in a general way into intercessions or petitions. We usually have quiet music behind the prayer time, though this depends on the particular community involved in the prayer.

We always conclude our collective prayer with the Lord's Prayer. This is the quintessential prayer of the church, the prayer of the baptized that is always present in the historic liturgy. It provides another strong touchstone of structure in contemporary worship. As a spiritual orienting marker, it centers our devotional life and the prayer life of the whole people. Sharing Jesus' prayer is sharing the very meaning of what it means to be a Christian in the world.

THE TABLE

In the Disciples' tradition, the theological center of the entire service is the Lord's table. And in terms of the flow of the service, it is to the table of our Lord that everything moves. The sacrament unites us not only with all of the other worship services within our particular congregation, but with the worship of the universal church. It creates unity among members of the body, recognizes the presence of Christ in our midst, and remembers who we are and whose we are.

Whatever else our worship contains, however innovative or different, this table is the structural center. It defines our very identity.

We are told that every time we eat the bread and drink the wine, we proclaim Christ's death until he comes. The table itself is an act of proclamation. Unlike other contemporary worship as practiced in other places, we would never imagine concealing, hiding, or displacing the supper for the sake of some sensitivity to seekers. This is exactly the word of the church that seekers need to hear. We place the transcendent mysteries before all who would come, knowing that they do not have them elsewhere. We invite them to be with us not in general, but in particular to a table that is able to satisfy the deep hungers of the heart. The best witness to the un-churched and irreligious alike is to be the church.

Though the essentials of the Lord's table are maintained throughout, the form of our table varies from our customary Disciples method of distribution of the elements. Instead of distributing the bread and wine in trays that circulate among the people, we ask people to come forward and receive communion by intinction—that is, tearing off a small piece of bread and dipping it into the cup. The ordained pastors preside at the table as links to the apostolic church of the ages, and after the pastor gives the invitation, the words of institution, and prayer of the table, the bread and chalice are left on the table. People come forward to the table with the pastors, who join the people and eat with them. This, for us, reinforces the unity of the one cup and the priesthood of all believers who share the feast together.

We sing as we commune, and regardless of the musical style that is employed, a spirit of reverence permeates the whole worshiping community. In the same way we have left ordinary time and space to enter the worship experience, so there lies an even deeper plane of the experience of God in holy communion. It is a hidden place within a hidden place. It is the body and blood of our Lord. It is the Lord's table.

THE SENDING

The final benediction, the blessing, both blesses the people and sends them forth as gospel people into the world. It most usually takes the form of a spoken blessing that is followed by an uplifting song of going forth.

After the song is completed, the band continues to play as the people mix, say farewell, and depart worship.

A NOTE ON BAPTISM

As the primary initiation rite into the body of Christ, baptism is an essential part of the worship of the people of God. When persons come to faith in the context of our contemporary worship service, we highlight the moment and make baptism the focus of our worship. For mature Christians, this acts as a tremendous reinforcement to their faith. In the baptism of any there is the remembrance of the many. In the case of searchers, baptism is a witness to the power of dying and rising in Christ, of God's graceful initiative, and our grateful response in obedience. Baptism is essentially a collective experience, to be shared by the whole people of God in the midst of Christian worship.

When it is time to baptize, the morning's theme wraps around the meaning of that act. The scriptures, message, and song accentuate the meaning of being a baptized community. When your contemporary service meets in a worship space without the means of baptizing, you may do as we do. We have a procession to the sanctuary, and gather around the baptistery, singing songs of baptism. After sharing the traditional scripture readings and prayers of baptism, we baptize in the threefold name of the trinity. We then return to our worship area and share the Lord's table with the newly baptized.

As in the case of the Lord's supper, we do everything in our power to lift up the powerful meanings that baptism holds in the midst of worship. Far from disguising or minimizing it in the interest of not confusing seekers, we instead let this act of the church teach the faith. And that is why we are here, is it not?

USING DRAMATIC MEDIA

Because a contemporary worship setting is more informal and generally interactive and expressive, it lends itself to the creative use of variable communication forms.

Many congregations have utilized drama as a means to provoke the questions of the day and set up the themes that will be addressed during the message. Drama often packs a pointed and graphic message into a relatively short duration of time. It is also in narrative form, which has the distinct advantage of reaching the life experience of the viewer.

Some contemporary worship utilizes a drama team that offers short vignettes every Sunday. In our services we have employed drama much more sparingly. Though we have seen it done effectively in other congregations, we have also witnessed very poor presentations that did not add to the power of the service. It all depends, of course, on the gifts in your community of faith. If your members have a highly gifted core of dramatists, then by all means employ them! If not, feel no obligation to include it. Whatever is offered must be of good, solid quality.

We have two cautions to offer in regard to the use of drama. First, if you do decide that you want to utilize drama as a regular part of your contemporary service, think twice about frequency. Familiarity may not breed contempt, but it will breed inattentiveness. If we have a skit every week, it becomes ordinary and expected. Why not use it more sparingly and expect it to bring more of a punch when it is used?

Second, be cautious about the commercial drama services that are available. Be selective. Much of the material we have viewed would be appropriate for senior high church camp and conference, but not for a broader and more mature congregation. Even seekers can see through the theological shallowness. The questions that are asked are generally too elementary. We have subscribed to drama services for a short period of time, only to throw away 90 percent of the material. If you have a talented writer in your congregation, you may do far better in asking this person to write material for you. The commercial services often serve up a theology you would rather not use.

Another auxiliary worship tool is that of creative media. We have used compelling selections of powerful documentaries or even movies on video tape. Those who are worshiping with you are accustomed to responding to television and cinema. There is often an immediate attentiveness that comes with this medium. If you use it, however, make sure it is a brief selection that truly illuminates some aspect of your theme or message. Also make sure that your technology is sufficient. Don't use a tape unless everyone can see and hear it easily. Test your equipment beforehand so that you are not wasting time trying to figure out how to use it.

An audio recording may also be shared. There is much material among contemporary secular artists that deals with the human condition, and some of it even hints at implicit religious themes. We have used a track from a CD or tape to lead into the message. Let the song ask the questions you would like for the congregation to ask. And make sure you print the words to the song in your bulletin. Join resources for both eye and ear for those who are visual and those who are auditory.

When Friends Leave

If we take effort to welcome the newly baptized or new members into the community, we also give special attention to the act of saying goodbye. In our extremely mobile society, church membership is fairly fluid. The church members, and those who are moving elsewhere, need to know that the leaving of any makes a difference to all. We all need closure as we exit one community and time in our lives and pass on to the next stage. The church needs to enact the meaning of that leaving in concrete rituals. One way to do this is to offer those who are leaving provisions for the journey.

In our community of faith, we mark this departure by the giving of a loaf of bread. In the "giving of the bread" we ask the pilgrims to come forward, remind the congregation that we break the bread every Sunday together and it exists as the highest sign of our unity, and then offer the bread with our blessings. The giving of a gift at the time of departure, especially this sort of a gift, marks the threshold for congregation and departing ones alike. There is both closure and opening to the future.

If you consider all of these things, you will be well on your way. But you have yet to address perhaps the most important practical dynamic that will either make or break your service—the way that you employ music. To that subject we now turn.

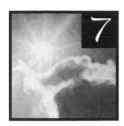

$\mathcal{I}$n the same way that a high setting of the sung mass is propelled forward by its choral settings, so contemporary worship moves on the wings of its music. Music creates movement in time through its sequence of sounds. It also transcends time through its ability to sweep the worshiper into a different state of mind and heart. Whether it is the text of *O God our Help* set to ST. ANNE'S ever-persistent quarter notes, the ethereal *Let All Mortal Flesh Keep Silence* floating on the rising and falling tune of PICARDY, any of the engaging new hymnody such as is written by Brian Wren or Tom Troeger, or a Psalm set in contemporary form by Amy Grant and Michael W. Smith in *Thy Word,* the soul is lifted beyond itself and finds communion with God.

As in so much other worship, music is the vehicle by which the gathered congregation is moved through the worshiping experience. It both shapes and creates the meanings and mood of the service. And, as anyone knows, it can either help or hinder.

What exactly is contemporary music? The linguistic root of the word contemporary is found in its parts: *with-time.* That is, it is a form that emerges from the creation of the present times. In this sense, all created music is contemporary.

The larger question becomes, "Created with the times *where?* " Is it contemporary music in the classic, country, rock, jazz, or folk pathways? When we start thinking about contemporary music, the issue of culture immediately comes to the fore. In our worship, what musical "cultures" will we be tapping? In which cultures do our people live, and where is our congregation socially located? In what part of the world do they live, and from what generation do they come? When they turn on the radio, or buy a CD, to what do they most often listen? Will they more often go to a rock concert or the symphony? And as we think about opening the windows of the church and inviting strangers to become friends, what different sounds shall greet their ears?

In our congregation we have answered that question with multiple services. Our traditional service is a "high culture" service that most often includes music from the broad classical repertoire. Our contemporary service is a "popular culture" service that is driven by an eclectic collection of music in the jazz, rock, folk, and world music idioms.

Choosing and Finding the Music

As you attempt to increase worship participation, you need to keep the congregation and its musical abilities in mind. After you select music that has a clear and focused message of faith, draw a distinction between the kind of music that might be offered as a special number by a group and the hymnody the congregation can sing. You must choose singable songs. This means a song should be clear and easy enough to sing after hearing it once or twice. The melody line needs to be fairly smooth, without too many awkward jumps that lose inexperienced singers. Good, solid, driving rhythm helps. And the singing range needs to be approachable, perhaps within the octave beginning with middle C.

Start with your hymnal! Most of the newly published hymnals, especially from the denominational publishing houses, have a wide variety of music that can easily be adapted for contemporary worship. This music often has chord symbols for use with accompanying rhythm instruments. Our music group uses no less than twenty-five songs from our new *Chalice Hymnal.*

Choose music from popular contemporary Christian music very selectively. The theology is frequently shallow and self-preoccupied. In addition, the music is fairly sanitized, canned, and sterile. In the midst of this wilderness, however, there are some genuine treasures. If you have the patience to discard twenty for every one you keep, it is a rich resource.

Some music companies produce hundreds, even thousands, of praise choruses. These are generally simple, repeated strains of scripture that the congregation sings over and over again. Their value is found not only in the appropriation of a short phrase of verse, but also in the physiological effect of repeated words and phrases. As a modern counterpart to meditative chant, they often elicit semi-trance states, such as one would encounter in the repetitive use of a mantra. Our preference is to use repeating choruses or chants from the contemplative tradition, and we have often used the compelling *Jesus, Remember Me and Eat This Bread* from Taize as we have communed. They are also quite moving as prologues or responses to community prayer.

Open your windows to the Christian music of other world cultures. Some of the most solid and engaging music for the church is being written in such places as Africa, Latin America, and the British Isles. Beautiful song in the contemplative tradition is coming from Iona in Scotland and Taize in France. Since Vatican II, the Catholic community has been producing reams of music for use in congregational life that you may adapt to your worship tradition. Some commercial companies are virtual repositories of the breadth of all this available music (See Appendix B).

THE MUSICAL LEADERSHIP STYLE

An essential feature of the Protestant Reformation was placing singing squarely in the midst of the congregation. As opposed to a presentational mode of choral performance in which some sang exclusively to or on behalf of others, the entire congregation was to be and do the liturgy of the Church.

In contemporary worship, much of the strength of the service comes with musical participation. Most of the music that takes place in the service should be sung by the people. Certainly, special solos or ensembles are appropriate, but they should not become normative. Too much of this creates passivity.

The musical leadership team is to teach, lead, and encourage the congregation to share in its own song. As they are a part of the roundtable of worship teams, they will attempt to choose music that is appropriate to theme, scripture, and message. The pastor and musical leadership must work together to assure sound theology and acceptable use of language. Musical forms often carry with them implicit theologies and views of human nature that are not acceptable. Regular communication with the pastor keeps the music on track with the whole service.

WHERE DO WE FIND THESE MUSICIANS?

Finding key musical leaders is one of your most difficult and important challenges. Each congregation will have to seek the charisms and gifts that reside in its membership. Usually you will not want to turn to your classical musicians who are providing music for the more traditional services. However gifted they are, most do not have the interest, motivation, or experience to play in the more popular idiom. Of course, this is not always the case, and some musicians are incredibly versatile and have a wide range of musical appreciation. In most instances, however, we would suggest that you go to the edges of your congregation and find musicians who are not participating in the mainstream music ministry of your congregation. In our experience, we found them there just waiting to launch into something quite new and nearer to their musical interests. Sometimes they just don't know what God has in store for them…at least until someone asks them. Find these people at the margins and then encourage them to use their hidden gifts for ministry.

Don't expect the perfect band, whatever that is. Instead, form something unique based on the gifts you have been given. One of the things we give thanks for is the diversity of gifts that have come together to make our musical leadership unique. We don't have the instrumentation to sound like anyone else. We sound like ourselves, and we rejoice that God has given this to us. Find the gifts and put them together into what God has for you.

Sometimes you just don't have it. Some congregations have a deficit of gifts in this kind of musical leadership. And in many cases, you must wait, and sometimes wait very patiently. As the process of our service and musical gifts continued, some members left and others came. Each time this happened, important shifts and changes took place. God is gracious, and you will receive what you need.

Though we always prefer live musicians leading the congregation in worship, as opposed to the artificial sound of a recording, you may need to rely on tapes or CDs to help you with your singing—at least for the time being. If you do, remember: The sound, however professional sounding, is artificial. People are surrounded by the artificial all the time. They need real folks singing and being with them. If you use pre-recorded music, you will be at the mercy of the form of the Christian message that happens to be represented there.

To Print or Project

For the music that is not in our hymnals, do we print it in the bulletin? Do we print nothing, and make transparencies and project all songs on a screen? We've tried it both ways, and both ways have advantages and disadvantages.

The advantages of projecting your words onto a screen are several: You get people's heads out of bulletins and looking upward. It helps singing, and it tends to open people to the larger community. It also uses less paper. You can make last-minute changes by simply choosing another pre-made slide or transparency.

On the other hand, if you don't have the right projection equipment, people strain to see the screen. Not everyone in the room will have the same quality of visibility. And a screen, or screens, sometimes communicates a kind of tackiness, a sort of boardroom presentation atmosphere. Some people do not find this worshipful.

The advantages of utilizing hymnals, songbooks, and printed words are also several: There is a portable versatility in distributing hymnals and songbooks, and they also provide the flexibility to make last-minute changes. Printed texts allow people to contemplate the words more carefully before and after singing a song. When a printed melody line accompanies the words, it serves as a very helpful aid in learning new music.

Also, the use of print medium eliminates both the time and expense of arranging for adequate projection systems, which can be very expensive.

The disadvantages of print medium include the requisite printing schedules and a lack of flexibility in last-minute changes, people burying their heads in their music rather than singing out, and shuffling paper rather than interacting with the gathered community.

Whatever option you choose in this regard, you must obtain the legal copyright permissions for both forms—projected or printed. Not only is this ethical, but congregations who through negligence have not done this, and have been caught, have paid dearly. (For copyright information, see Appendix B.)

PLUGGED OR UNPLUGGED?

Should we use amplification? Do we need mikes and a sound system for the musical group? It all depends on the size and nature of the room in which your worship takes place.

Some folks are too hasty to amplify just because they think it needs to be done. There are some rooms with naturally fine acoustics and you need very little artificial amplification. In fact, the less intrusive amplification the better in terms of encouraging the congregation to sing. Amplification should only augment sound in order that it be heard, not so that it dominates. Our musical group has played in many different locations, each of which called for different kinds of sound. In playing in a large hall, with lots of "dead" surfaces, amplification becomes essential. On the other hand, if you are singing for a group of fifty in a church fellowship hall, your needs become significantly less. If your musical leadership uses amplifiers for electric or electronic instruments, you will need to balance that sound with the sound of the voices. Acoustic instruments will blend with voices much more easily, if the location allows for them to be heard. The existing sound system in your sanctuary or fellowship hall may be more harmful than helpful to your sound. You do need to be heard, and in time, you may do well to purchase a portable sound system that will allow you flexibility, resonance, and high quality. Whatever else you do, have someone with a good ear listen to sound levels "out front." Distortion, or volumes that are too soft or too loud, will detract from your message, impact, and ultimate communication with the congregation.

CONCLUSION

So you are thinking about contemporary worship? Good! Don't be unnecessarily daunted by the task. But then again...

> know why you are doing what you are doing
> do your homework
> plan carefully
> organize well
> design a process that includes the whole
>   congregation

dare to have theological integrity
choose the right time and space
keep an eye to visitors
dare to be a community of word and sacrament
keep it simple but not simplistic
discover and create rituals
foster Christian community
and find music that is compelling.

Then take your place in the company of those who have shared in this blessing through the centuries. Remember: Do not become discouraged if your well-meaning plans do not immediately materialize as you have hoped and expected. Let your failures, setbacks, and unanticipated surprises be the occasion for growth, learning, and change. Pioneers have always faced the challenges that accompany the charting of new territory. Never forget that you are surrounded and sustained by the love that will not let you go, and Christian friends who dare to go there with you.

# Appendix A

A Sample Order of Service

The Gathering of God's People
Sharing in Song
(Songs not in the hymnal are printed in the
insert.)
A Time of Greeting and Welcome
Concerns of the Community

The Word for the Day
Scripture Session
The Message
The People Respond in Song
(If you wish to make a commitment to God in
Jesus Christ,
or become a member of our community of faith,
come forward now!)

The Prayers of the People
The Sharing of our Joys and Concerns
The Pastoral Prayer
The Lord's Prayer
(Words to the prayer are printed here.)

The Great Thanksgiving
The Gifts of the People
The Table of our Lord
The Invitation, Prayer, and Words of Institution
(All those who are baptized Christians are invited
    to partake,
regardless of denominational affiliation.
Come forward up the center aisle, dip the bread
    into the cup,
partake, and return by side aisle.)
The Song of Communion

The Sending Forth
The Blessing and Song of Sending

# Appendix B

RESOURCES

Some of Our Favorite Musical Sources

Chalice Hymnal. (St. Louis: Chalice Press, 1995)
This most recent hymnbook of the Christian
Church (Disciples of Christ) incorporates a rich
diversity of hymnody, including a variety of ethnic
traditions, the best of contemporary music, psalms with
sung responses, and language that enriches the way in
which God is represented. Chords most usually
accompany the hymns where such indications are helpful.

To order: Chalice Press
P.O. Box 179
St. Louis, Missouri 63166

Gather, Second Edition, Vols. 1 and 2. (Chicago:
GIA Publications, Inc., 1994)
The second generation of a 1988 hymnal of the
same name, *Gather* is a broad collection of liturgical
service music, hymnody, and song. The orientation of
its music is collective, to be used in corporate worship.
The present edition is simple enough to be accompanied by piano alone, though guitar chords are included
throughout.

To order: GIA Publications
7404 South Mason Avenue
Chicago, Illinois, 60638

Global Songs, Local Voices. (Minneapolis, Minnesota: Bread for the Journey, 1995)

A product of the group Bread for the Journey, this collection brings the resources of the global Christian community to the United States. This edition includes keyboard, words, and chords, and it is accompanied by background and performance notes for each song.

> To order: Bread for the Journey
> P.O. Box 141149
> Minneapolis, MN 55414

Glory & Praise, Vols. 1 and 2. (Phoenix: North American Liturgy Resources, 1980)

Published as a keyboard version with chords as well as a congregational hymnbook with melody, words, and no chords, these songbooks gather together the best liturgical music from the contemporary Catholic tradition.

> To order: North American Liturgy
> Resources
> 10802 North 23rd Avenue
> Phoenix, Arizona 85029

Many and Great. (Chicago: The Iona Community/Wild Goose Publications, 1990)

Twenty-five songs from the world church that have stood the test of time in their own locales include performance notes, guitar chords where appropriate, and English translations.

To order: GIA Publications, Inc.
7404 South Mason Avenue
Chicago, Illinois 60638

Psalms of Patience, Protest and Praise. (Scotland:
The Iona Community, 1993)
These metrical settings of the paraphrased psalms
by John Bell offer worshipers the broad range of divine
reality and human condition that only the psalms may
bring. The collection provides keyboard, words, and
chords, and helpful commentary for each psalm.

To order: GIA Publications, Inc.
7404 South Mason Avenue
Chicago, Illinois 60638

Songs and Prayers from Taizé. (Taizé, France:
Ateliers et Presses de Taizé, 1991)
This collection of responses, litanies, acclamations,
and canons in basic Latin text and English was written
for use in the Taizé community. Melody and chords
accompany the text throughout, and a more complete
keyboard edition with solo instruments is available. The
meditative quality of the repetitive chants fosters a deep
experience of prayer.

To order: GIA Publications, Inc.
7404 South Mason Avenue
Chicago, Illinois 60638

Spirit Calls...Rejoice! (Burnsville, Minnesota: Prince of Peace Publishing, Inc., 1991)

The musical fare of this collection is solid, though because all of the music and words are composed by the same musicians, there is sometimes a certain sameness to all of the works. Though some of the music is quite difficult for congregational singing, the songbook contains many great finds. It comes with a keyboard edition with chords, and a congregational songbook with melody and words.

> To order: Prince of Peace
> Publishing, Inc.
> 200 East Licollet Boulevard
> Burnsville, Minnesota
> 55337

Thuma Mina: International Ecumenical Hymnbook. (Munich, Germany: Strube Verlag, 1995)

This is a collection of Christian song from the ecumenical church around the world. The texts most often come in the language from which the song originated, but English is almost always provided as one of the options. Melody, words, and chords provided.

> To order: Strube Verlag GmbH
> PettenkoferstraBe24
> 80336 Munich
> Germany

COPYRIGHT INFORMATION

With an increasing number of lawsuits being brought against churches, the risk of copyright violation has become exceedingly high. In addition, Christians respect the rights of those who create on behalf of the church and for its benefit.

Copyright law exists to protect the commercial value of copyrighted work for those who depend upon it for their livelihood. The law grants exclusive rights of ownership to the *owner of a copyright* (which is not the same as the *publisher*). If a selection is in *Public Domain* (PD), it is no longer protected by copyright and no permission for use need be obtained. PD is defined as an uncopyrighted work or a work for which the copyright term has expired. Arrangements of PD work are copyrightable.

Though there are fair-use copyright exemptions in remarkable circumstances, churches must remember that they may not reproduce any copyrighted material in any form for any reason. This includes projecting words of music on screens, printing words of songs in bulletins, copying anthems for choirs, copying hymns for congregations, or assembling compilations of songs for personalized songbooks.

You may obtain permission for use by means of two ways:

1. Write directly to the holder of the copyright and request permission.

2. Purchase a church blanket license. A copyright license provides churches permission to print texts and music in any form. The annual license fee is generally based on the size of the church.

To Obtain Rights to Perform Music in a Religious Setting

Christian Copyright Licensing International
(CCLI)
17201 NE Sacramento Street
Portland, OR 97230
(800) 234-2446

Broadcast Music, Inc. (BMI)
320 West 57th Street
New York, NY 10019
(212) 586-2000

SESAC, Inc.
421 West 54th Street
New York, NY 10019
(212) 586-3450

American Society of Composers
Authors & Publishers (ASCAP)
One Lincoln Plaza
New York, NY 10023
(212) 595-3050

To Locate a Copyright Owner of a Work

National Music Publishers' Association, Inc.
  (NMPA)
711 3rd Avenue, 8th Floor
New York, NY 10017
(212) 370-5330

Music Publishers' Association of the United States
  (MPA)
c/o NMPA/HFA
711 3rd Avenue, 8th Floor
New York, NY 10017
(212) 370-5330

Church Music Publishers Association
PO Box 158992
Nashville, TN 37215
(615) 791-0273

U.S. Copyright Office
(202) 707-3000

Canadian Consumer and Corporate Affairs
Bureau of Intellectual Property
(613) 997-1936

ABOUT THE AUTHORS

Tim and Kathy Carson are life-long Disciples and are currently members of Webster Groves Christian Church in St. Louis, Missouri. They are both involved in the leadership of the contemporary worship service. Tim is the senior minister of the congregation and has served in that capacity for the last six years. Kathy is on the staff of the Division of Higher Education of the Christian Church (Disciples of Christ) and serves the Webster Groves Christian Church in many capacities, especially in the area of music and worship.

Tim holds a B.Music Ed. from Drury College, Springfield, Missouri; the M.Div. from Brite Divinity School, Fort Worth, Texas; and the D.Min. in pastoral theology from Eden Theological Seminary in St. Louis, Missouri. Kathy holds an B.S. in education from Southeast Missouri State University in Cape Girardeau, Missouri.

Both of the Carsons have been very active in regional and general ministries of the Disciples as well as the life of their local congregations. They have one daughter, Savannah, who loves her long-haired guinea pig, Pocahontas.